IN THE POCKET

JAZZ SNARE DRUM SOLOS
WITH THE LEGENDS

Play along with Chick, Keith, Bird, Ella & more

RUDIMENTAL CHOPS NOT REQUIRED TO PLAY THIS BOOK

by
Albie Berk

TABLE OF CONTENTS

INTRODUCTION

"You are so in the pocket." Words every musician loves to hear. But what does it really mean?

In The Pocket: Something or someone playing in such a way that the groove is very solid and has a great feel.

Groove: When all players are in sync and the music has an effortless and exciting sound. The "lock" between members of a rhythm section playing well together.

Feel: The overall emotional impact the music is making. In jazz, we use words like really cookin', swingin', burnin'.

What makes this book different is that you will be playing along with the soloists, not the drummers.

The snare drum solos in this book were inspired by and based on performances by some of my favorite jazz artists. Each solo is based on the melody and instrumental solos of jazz legends like Chick Corea, Keith Jarrett, Ella Fitzgerald, Charlie Parker, and others. These recordings, some of which date back to the 1940's, are classics. The versions are all available on YouTube and all streaming services. Be sure to use the recordings that I reference. You will also be playing along with great rhythm sections that define the phrase in the pocket.

For rock drummers, this book can be a bridge to developing a jazz feel by playing along with these greats.

At first glance the solos may appear simple. Remember, this IS NOT a book of rudimental etudes. Of course, as they are the basis of all drumming, the rudiments are referenced here, and you should be studying them as well. These solos are to guide you and help you develop a jazz feel. Ultimately, this is a book to help your improvisational skills.

This book works on many levels and can help you to:

- Improve your sight-reading while playing along with brilliant solos.
- Play alongside the recordings of great drummers.
- Learn jazz standards.
- Create your own stickings and dynamics to go with the tracks.
- Use "space" in a solo and allow the music to breathe.
- Develop your feel and groove as a basis for all your playing.
- Raise your improvisation skills through guided solos that encourage creativity

HOW TO PRACTICE THIS BOOK

Each song will have two solos. One is just the melody and the improvisation. The other is the melody and improvisation surrounded by fills that I created. The sequence of practicing these would be:

- Start by playing the melody in solo one.
- Progress to solo two, integrating fills around the melody.
- Revisit solo one and add your improvisational fills.
- As you gain confidence, tackle the solos at their recommended tempos.
- Elevate your experience by playing along with the tracks linked to each solo.

ADDITIONAL PRACTICING IDEAS

- Use a metronome when you can.
- Listen to the recommended track for that solo and follow the music.
- Read the solo at a comfortable tempo until feeling good about it.
- Play the solo at the recommended tempo.
- Play the solo with the track.
- Sometimes the solo will end but the music will continue. Try to keep going and jam with the artists.
- If you are playing these at a drum set, try adding your bass drum and hi hat when you're ready.

You may want to get right at it or start simple, by playing the solos slowly. If you become frustrated while practicing, cut back a little to where you were having some fun and work up from the there.

I am not including a lot of stickings or dynamics. Occasionally I'll put in some stickings or accent marks when I think it will help guide you. This is jazz so I want to allow for creativity and for each drummer to feel the music the way they do. As you play these etudes, your interpretation will probably change. Just make the solos your own and have a blast!

MY GOAL FOR THIS BOOK

The purpose of this book is to get you to emulate the pocket by playing along with these jazz legends and then be able to bring that feeling to any musical situation. It's all about knowing when you are in the pocket and how to get there if you're not. I have always believed that the best way to learn things is to have them presented in a fun and joyful way. I hope this book does that for you and makes you more than just a better drummer - a better musician.

SPECIAL THANKS

Ron Tierno - For writing his book *The Melodic Snare Drummer*. My inspiration for this book came from Ron.

Jerry Kalaf - A great drummer, educator and friend who was a sounding board for this entire process. From Finale help to playing through the solos.

Doug Walter - For his "green visor" editing and being so generous with his time.

Meridith - For having some great ideas and being totally supportive and helpful throughout the creation of this book

ACKNOWLEDGEMENT FOR NO REASON WHATSOEVER

Tom Hanks (Because everybody likes Tom Hanks)

Keith Jarrett

Keith Jarrett is an American pianist and composer. Jarrett started his career with Art Blakey and later moved on to play with Charles Lloyd and Miles Davis. Since the early 1970s, Jarrett has also been a group leader and solo performer in jazz, jazz fusion, and classical music.

Play along with:
"Bye Bye Blackbird"
Keith Jarrett - Live at the Deer Head Inn
ECM Records 1992

Keith Jarrett - Piano
Gary Peacock - Bass
Paul Motian - Drums

Keith's playing is bursting with spontaneity. I stayed close to what he played and tried to stay in his style. I added accents to help point the way. After a few listenings you should fall right into what he is doing.

Listen to how Paul Motian interacts. Since his days with the great Bill Evans trio, Paul has been one of the most influential drummers of the last 60 years.

To quote my friend Jerry Kalaf:

"When Keith plays four quarter notes he's playing a lot more than four quarter notes."

Bye Bye Blackbird - (melody)

Keith Jarrett

"Live at the Deerhead Inn"

Chorus 1

Chorus 2

Bye Bye Blackbird

Bye Bye Blackbird

Bye Bye Blackbird

13

Bye Bye Blackbird - (with fills)

Keith Jarrett

"Live at the Deerhead Inn"

Chorus 1

Chorus 2

Bye Bye Blackbird

Chorus 3

Chorus 4

Chorus 5

Chorus 6

DAVE BRUBECK QUARTET
featuring Paul Desmond

Dave was an American jazz pianist and composer. His work is characterized by unusual time signatures and superimposing contrasting rhythms, meters, and tonalities. The recording, Time Out, was groundbreaking for its day. The song Take Five, written by saxophonist Paul Desmond went on to become the biggest-selling jazz single of all time.

Play along with:
"Take Five"
Time Out
Columbia Records 1959

Dave Brubeck – Piano
Paul Desmond – Alto Saxophone
Eugene Wright – Bass
Joe Morello – Drums

This snare solo stays pretty close to Paul Desmond's performance. The arrangement doesn't lend itself to fill-ins or additional improvisation, so I only created one solo. Playing along while listening to Joe's flawless drumming should really be fun!

Joe Morello's drumming sounds natural and effortless even in this odd time signature. Joe was always a student of drumming and went on to write several great method books. Some of his notable students are Danny Gottlieb, Max Weinberg, John Riley, Jon Hazilla and others. Please listen to the entire Time Out record and any others you can find of Joe. He should be on every drummers "must listen to" list.

Take Five - (melody)
Dave Brubeck Quartet
"Time Out"

Joe Morello

Charlie Parker

Nicknamed "Bird", was an American jazz saxophonist, band leader and composer. Parker was a highly influential soloist and leading figure in the development of bebop, a form of jazz characterized by fast tempos, virtuosic technique, and advanced harmonies.

Play along with:
"Donna Lee"
Charlie Parker All Stars
Savoy Records 1947

Charlie Parker - Alto Sax
Miles Davis - Trumpet
Bud Powell - Piano
Tommy Potter - Bass
Max Roach - Drums

On this snare solo I am sticking very close to the recording. This is bebop at its best and just playing along with Bird, Miles and Bud is a real learning experience. Pay attention to Max Roach's groundbreaking drumming. He was one of the main contributors to the development of bebop. Bebop drummers tend to play with a more complex and syncopated style, creating a more rhythmic and dynamic interplay with the other musicians.

Donna Lee - (melody)

Charlie Parker All-Stars

Donna Lee

Donna Lee

Donna Lee

Max Roach

Donna Lee - (with fills)

Charlie Parker All-Stars

Donna Lee

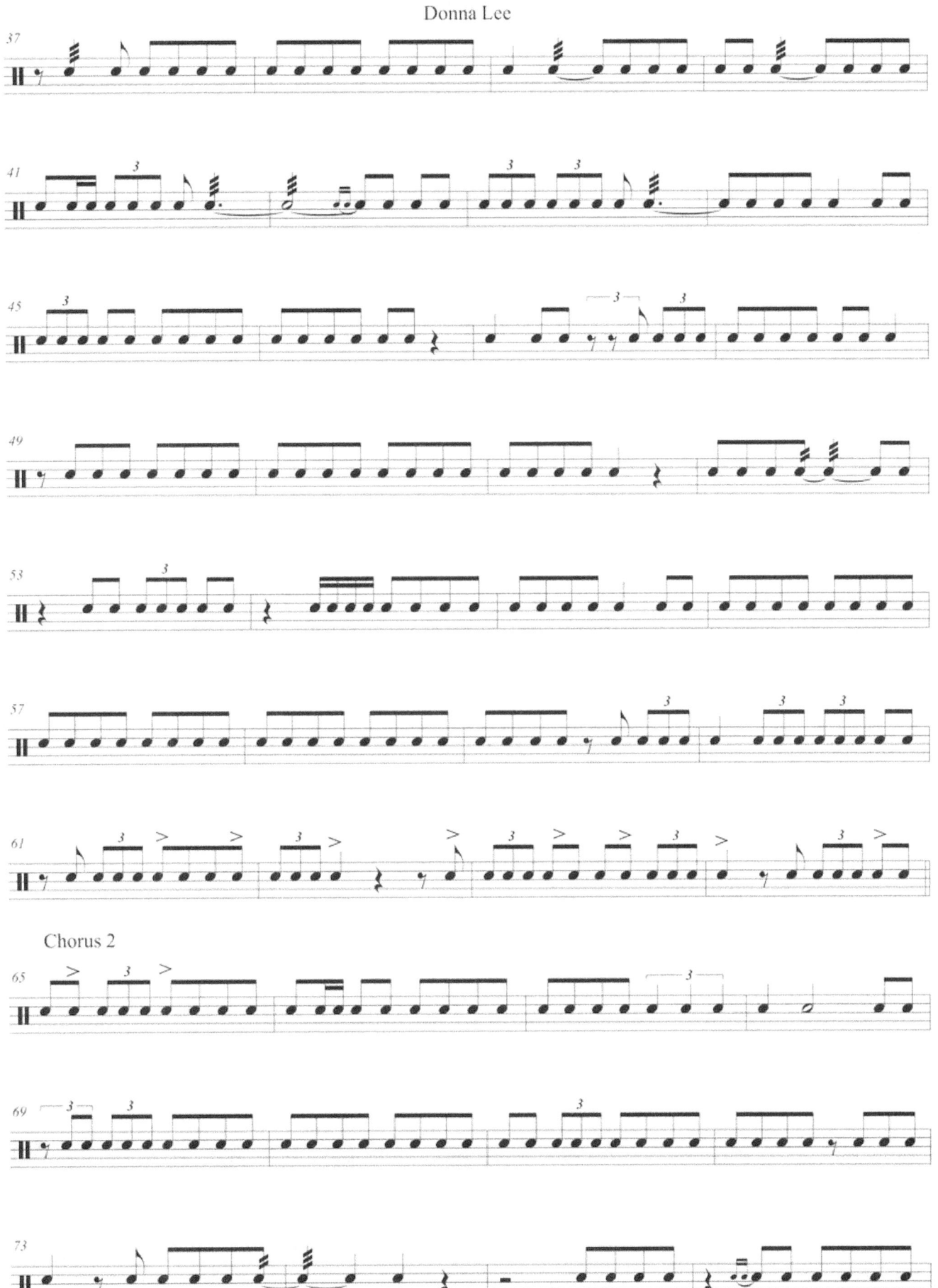

Donna Lee

Donna Lee

Melody

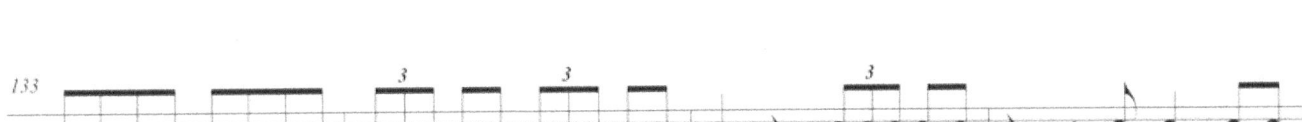

Ella Fitzgerald

An American jazz singer, sometimes referred to as the "First Lady of Song."
She was noted for her purity of tone, impeccable diction, phrasing, timing,
intonation, and a "horn-like" improvisational ability known as scat singing.

Play along with:
'Blue Skies"
Ella Fitzgerald - Get Happy
Verve Records 1959

Please note: A dot above a note = "Not Swung"

This is a stellar performance of an American Songbook standard. A great
artist knows how to build a solo. Ella's goes from from long phrases to
syncopated bursts and back again. I kept the drum solo pretty close to what
she does as she is really in the pocket!

This recording is acknowledged as one of her most impressive scat singing
performances.

Blue Skies - (melody)

Ella Fitzgerald
"Get Happy"

Ella Scatting

Blue Skies

Chorus 2

36

Blue Skies - (with fills)

Ella Fitzgerald
"Get Happy"

Ella Scatting

Blue Skies

Chorus 3

DEXTER GORDON

Dexter was an American jazz tenor saxophonist, composer, and bandleader. In the 1940's, along with Charlie Parker and Dizzy Gillespie he was a prominent figure in the emerging bebop movement. Dexter has a big, breathy sound and is a master at blending bebop with some real emotion. Playing along with him should present some new challenges.

Play along with:
"Blue Bossa"
Biting The Apple
Blue Note Records 1978

Dexter Gordon – Tenor Saxophone
Barry Harris – Piano
Sam Jones – Bass
Al Foster – Drums

For over 50 years, Al Foster has been a major innovator in the world of jazz. He has played with everyone from Dexter Gordon to Bill Evans to Sting. To quote Miles Davis, "...He had such a groove and he would just lay it right in there. For what I wanted in a drummer, Al Foster had all of it."

Blue Bossa (melody)

Dexter Gordon
"Bite The Apple"

Blue Bossa

Blue Bossa

46

Blue Bossa

Blue Bossa

Chorus 9

Keep playing along

Al Foster

Blue Bossa (with fills)

Dexter Gordon
"Bite The Apple"

Blue Bossa

Chorus 1

Chorus 2

Chorus 3

Blue Bossa

Chorus 4

Chorus 5

Blue Bossa

Chorus 6

Chorus 7

Chorus 8

R R L L R R L L

Chet Baker

An American jazz trumpeter and vocalist. He was known for major innovations in cool jazz. Chet earned much attention and critical praise through the 1950s, particularly for albums featuring his vocals.

Play along with:
"Autumn Leaves"
Chet Baker - She Was Too Good to Me
CTI Records 1974

Bob James - Piano
Ron Carter - Bass
Steve Gadd -Drums
Paul Desmond - Alto Sax

Chet is a unique soloist. His playing on Autumn Leaves sets the standard for "West Coast cool." In contrast to Chet's laid back style we have Steve Gadd's rolling triplets and great light touch generating lots of energy. I have merged Chet's playing and Steve's together in the snare drum solo to show off both artists.

Autumn Leaves - (melody)

Chet Baker
"She Was Too Good to Me"

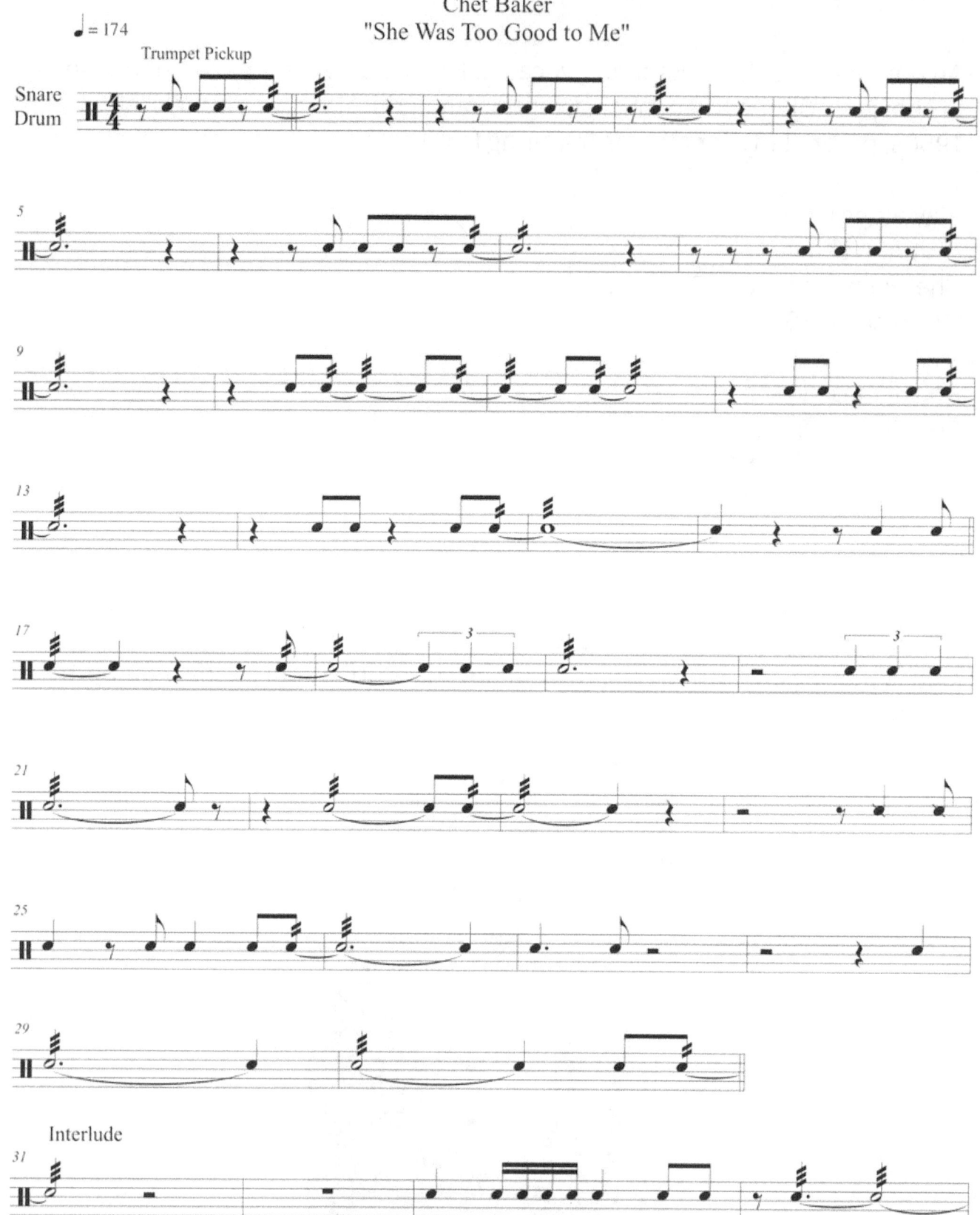

Chorus 1

Interlude 2

Chorus 2

Interlude

Continue Playing with Sax Solo

Steve Gadd

Autumn Leaves - (with fills)

Chet Baker
"She Was Too Good to Me"

Autumn Leaves

Chorus Two

Interlude

Continue Playing with Sax Solo

Chick Corea

Chick was a highly influential American jazz pianist, composer, and bandleader. In the late 1960's he was on the forefront of the birth of jazz fusion with his group Return To Forever. He went on to win 27 Grammy Awards.

Play along with:
"Matrix"
Now He Sings, Now He Sobs
Solid State Records 1968

Chick Corea - Piano
Miroslav Vitous - Bass
Roy Haynes - Drums

Now He Sings, Now He Sobs ranks as one of the most influential piano trio records of all time.

Roy Haynes sounds like he's dancing on the cymbals and snare composing his own counter rhythms to Chick. Roy is one of the masters and should be part of your normal listening.

The solo is "almost" even eighths. I have matched Chick's soloing with an occasional fill by Roy. There is a beautiful looseness to this track that might take playing it a few times to really get on it. The time is well spent. It can only make you a better musician.

Matrix - (melody)

Chick Corea
"Now He Sings, Now He Sobs"

Chorus 2

Chorus 3

Chorus 4

Chorus 5

Chourus 12

Roy Haynes

Matrix - (with fills)

Chick Corea
"Now He Sings, Now He Sobs"

Chorus 9

Chorus 10

Chorus 11

Chorus 12

Albie was born in Brooklyn, New York, and currently lives in Los Angeles. He graduated from the Juilliard School of Music, where he studied with Morris Goldenberg and Buster Bailey. His other teachers included Joel Rothman, Ted Reed, Sonny Igoe and Ed Shaughnessy. Over the years, he has been the personal touring drummer for such people as Debbie Reynolds, Tony Danza, Joel Grey, Barbara Cook, Anthony Newley, Rita Moreno, Connie Francis, and Suzanne Somers, and has been Michael Feinstein's drummer for more than 30 years, both on the road and locally.

In Los Angeles, he has worked on the Academy Awards, The Carol Burnett Show, and many musicals, cartoons and other in-town shows and events, including The Los Angeles Philharmonic.

Albie played on Bette Midler's movie version of the Broadway show "Gypsy," Barry Manilow's gold record, "Singing with the Big Bands" and on the "Michael Feinstein with the Israel Philharmonic" CD. He is currently the drummer in the Pasadena Symphony and Pops.

The scope of his career has encompassed playing for individual entertainers, shows, recordings, choreographers, telethons, films and everything in between, all of which require having a broad frame of reference and being able to play many styles at a high level. And he continues to have a great time doing it.

Amid all this activity, Albie still finds time to get together and play jazz with friends and work in the local club scene.

> *"Albie, I really think there is a jazz drummer hiding in there trying to get out."*
> Piano legend - Alan Broadbent

Please feel free to write me with any
comments or suggestions you might have.
www.inthepocketpublishing.net
albieberk@gmail.com